T0198377

THE FOUR LAWS OF LOVE

———

DISCUSSION GUIDE

INTRODUCTION

The universal need of all human beings on planet earth is love. It doesn't matter your age, sex or ethnicity. Our Creator wired us to love and be loved. It is our greatest need and desire. It is the inspiration of our grandest dreams. It is at the core of our hopes for the future—we just want to be loved.

God created love and marriage and He created laws to guide and guard them. When God's laws are honored, marriage is the safest relationship on the earth, and the love we need is promoted and protected within it. When God's laws are violated—knowingly or unknowingly—it diminishes, or even destroys, the environment necessary for true and lasting love.

God would never create anything to harm us. He is a good God of love and order. He never creates anything that is chaotic or inherently evil. Everything He does is done with perfection and with our best interests in mind. This is also true of marriage. He created it to bless and fulfill us. God made marriage as the primary human relationship to give us the ability to fulfill our need for love on the deepest level. Many people are afraid of marriage as an institution and have decided to avoid it altogether. They have experienced or witnessed so much pain related to bad marriages that their fears of failure in marriage have exceeded their dreams of success.

However, God created marriage and the laws that govern it. God's four laws of love make the difference between success and failure in marriage. They guarantee the love we seek and need so badly will be present and protected for a lifetime. The four laws of love are found in a small portion of scripture in the second chapter of Genesis. *Therefore a man shall leave his father and mother and be joined to his wife, and they shall become one flesh. And they were both naked, the man and his wife, and were not ashamed* (Genesis 2:24-25, NKJV).

When people understand and apply the laws of love to their marriage relationships, they are transformed. Chaos becomes order. Pain becomes pleasure. Hopelessness becomes passion. Wherever you are in your marriage journey, I pray this study encourages and enlightens you. May the Lord give you the marriage of your dreams!

Blessings,

Jimmy Evans

HOW TO USE THIS DISCUSSION GUIDE

1. **The Discussion Guide** Read through each session together as a couple or with your group. The verses and key thoughts are great take-aways to meditate on.
2. **Watch the XO Now Online Videos** Jimmy Evans provides a short time of teaching for each session. Watch the video that corresponds with your session.
3. **Questions & Activation** Work through some of the questions with your spouse and/or group. Then set aside a time to do the "Just Between Us" part together as a couple.

HOW TO WATCH THE XO NOW ONLINE VIDEOS

1. This discussion guide comes with **One Free Month of XO Now!** Go to **xomarriage.com/now** and enter the coupon code: **LASTINGLOVE** during checkout.
2. Log into your XO Now account and search 'Four Laws of Love' to find *The Four Laws of Love* videos.

*If you already have an XO Now account you can still use the Free Month off coupon by going to xomarriage.com/now/myaccount, clicking Edit Subscription, then Apply coupon, entering the coupon code and clicking update subscription. The discount will be applied to your next invoice.

**This coupon only works if you sign up through our website. It will not work if you try to sign up through the apps (Apple, Google, Roku, Amazon) or if you have previously signed up through the apps.

CONTENTS

DEMYSTIFYING MARRIAGE

"Therefore a man shall leave his father and mother and be joined to his wife, and they shall become one flesh. And they were both naked, the man and his wife, and were not ashamed."

GENESIS 2:24–25 (NKJV)

God designed marriage to operate as the most important human relationship in our lives, and He designed the four laws of love to create, build, and maintain the marriage relationship. The marriage relationship only works when it is in first place in our lives. This is the law of priority. The second law is the law of pursuit. In order for love to be created and maintained in marriage, you have to work at it. The law of partnership means there is equal partnership in the marriage and no one is dominating the other. The fourth law is the law of purity. God created Adam and Eve naked and they were unashamed, until sin entered the picture.

As God designed it, marriage is the safest relationship on earth. And people fall in love when they put each other first in their lives, meet each other's needs, they don't dominate each other, and they are careful with their actions. When we follow the four laws of love it resurrects and heals our marriage. We have a loving and forgiving God, and it is never too late to follow the four laws of love. When we do marriage God's way, we are guaranteed success.

"As you commit to establish and protect the proper priorities of your marriage, you will find there are frequent challenges, but also awesome rewards. You just cannot improve on God's design. He made marriage as something sacred and beautiful, and it will stay that way if we prioritize it properly." – Jimmy Evans, The Four Laws of Love | Pg. 14

AS GOD
DESIGNED IT,
MARRIAGE IS
THE SAFEST
RELATIONSHIP
ON EARTH.

Watch "Session 1 – Demystifying Marriage" on XO Now.

DISCUSSION QUESTIONS

1. What are the top three priorities in your life? How do you treat your priorities differently?

2. God designed marriage to operate as the most important human relationship in our lives. How would this look in your everyday life?

3. Did your parents model marriage as happy and fulfilled or as unhappy and disappointing?

4. How did your parents' example influence your view of the laws of priority and partnership in marriage?

5. Which law do you think you are succeeding at? What law do you need to work on the most?

6. If you have kids, what type of marriage do you want to model for them? If you don't have kids, how do you want your marriage to reflect God to the world?

JUST BETWEEN US

This week, write your spouse a love letter expressing to them how you desire to re-prioritize your life so that the marriage is first. List one specific way that you wish to reprioritize your life in order for your marriage to flourish.

PROTECTING THE PRIORITY OF YOUR MARRIAGE

"But seek first His kingdom and His righteousness;
and all these things shall be added to you."

MATTHEW 6:33 (NASB)

One of the reasons we fall in love is because priority says, I choose you above any other pursuit in my life. Many fights in marriage happen when something else takes priority in marriage. Prioritized communication is essential in a healthy marriage. Husbands and wives need undisturbed face to face time daily to communicate. Friends, parents, children, and social media must remain in their place, which is secondary to your marriage.

Romance protects the priority of marriage. Romance means meeting an unspoken need in your spouse's life and in their language. Protecting the priority of our marriage means we prioritize communication, keep our spouse first place in our lives, and we are intentionally romantic.

"The Five Pillars of Communication are: The Right Tone, Enough Time, Trust, Truth, and Teamwork." – Jimmy Evans, The Four Laws of Love | Pg.26

PUTTING YOUR
MARRIAGE
FIRST MEANS
MEETING
YOUR SPOUSE'S
NEEDS BEFORE
THEY ASK.

Watch "Session 2 - Protecting the Priority of Your Marriage" on XO Now.

DISCUSSION QUESTIONS

1. What does it mean to re-prioritize your life in order to have a healthy marriage?

2. What are some things in life that tend to compete for our time, attention, and priority? How can we be vigilant about keeping boundaries on those things?

3. Why is it important to prioritize 30–60 minutes for daily communication? How have you seen this have a positive impact in your marriage?

4. On a personal note, what are some specific things that your spouse does that make you feel prioritized?

5. What are some specific things you can do to make your spouse feel prioritized?

6. Why is empathy (thinking about your spouse's needs) one of the most important areas in marriage to keep alive?

JUST BETWEEN US

You can't microwave communication, and nothing can substitute for it. Every couple needs between thirty and sixty minutes daily for personal communication. Together, decide on a set time each day when you can share your hearts and have meaningful communication and then do it.

THE SERVANT RULES

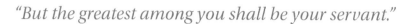

"But the greatest among you shall be your servant."

MATTHEW 23:11 (NASB)

The law of pursuit can be summarized by this simple truth that marriage only works when you work at it. We marry because there are needs that we have that we can't meet. In marriage, when we serve each other, we meet each other's needs. Serve what your spouse needs in spite of what you need, want, or understand. When your spouse tells you what they want or expresses their need, take note and serve them in that way.

Enjoy serving your spouse and do it with a joyful attitude. Reject score keeping and do what you do with a spirit of grace and faith. Vigilantly protect the time and energy necessary to serve your spouse. Expect to be blessed and don't get discouraged and give up. God's plan for marriage is that two humble-hearted, servant-spirited people who are both submitted to God and each other, love each other as equals.

"When our spouses have an unmet need, we should be there with a good attitude to serve them." – Jimmy Evans, The Four Laws of Love | Pg. 83

THE GREATEST
MARRIAGE ON EARTH
IS TWO SERVANTS
IN LOVE.

XO ▷ Watch "Session 3 - The Servant Rules" on XO Now.

DISCUSSION QUESTIONS

1. How is rejecting "score keeping" a way of serving your spouse? What does it mean to "Do the right thing first?"

2. How can serving one another help your marriage?

3. Think of a time in your marriage when your spouse served you or did something with a servant heart. Share this example and how it made you feel.

4. What is one act of service that makes you feel loved by your spouse?

5. What does serving with a great attitude look like?

6. Ask your spouse two specific ways you can express love to them through serving.

JUST BETWEEN US

Find a way to serve your spouse in a unique way. Hide love notes for them around the house. Bring home their favorite dessert. Do one of their chores for them. Make them feel special and tell them how much you love them.

MARRIED ON PURPOSE

"Where there is no vision, the people are unrestrained,
But happy is he who keeps the law."

PROVERBS 29:18 (NASB)

We need God's vision so that we can be married on purpose. God loves you and He has a wonderful plan for your marriage. Success never happens by accident. We have to choose a positive purpose for our marriage and commit to it.

Vision retreats are helpful for taking your marriage to the next level. Every year, you need to be getting away alone to talk and pray about every area in your marriage. Start by submitting your marriage to God. When you find agreement regarding each area, write it down and this is your vision for the next year. Be married on purpose and pursue each other intentionally.

"Vision retreats get better every year because you learn how to do them, and as time goes on you aren't dealing with as big of issues as in the beginning. So, don't get discouraged, and don't give up."
– Jimmy Evans, The Four Laws of Love | Pg.100

WHEN WE DON'T AGREE ON A SINGULAR VISION FOR OUR MARRIAGE, DIVISION IS INEVITABLE. INTENTIONALLY PURSUE GOD'S VISION FOR YOUR MARRIAGE.

Watch "Session 4 – Married On Purpose" on XO Now.

DISCUSSION QUESTIONS

1. What does it take to come to an agreement on important issues?

2. What does it mean to have a vision for your marriage?

3. How do we purposely pursue God's vision for our marriage and what would this look like in our marriage if we were more intentional about pursuing God's vision?

4. How would a vision retreat affect your own marriage and do you think it would help you and your spouse to connect?

5. Read Habakkuk 2:2. What do you think God's purpose is for bringing you and your spouse together?

6. What would you have to do to plan and do a vision retreat? Are there any obstacles? If so, what are some creative solutions to those obstacles?

JUST BETWEEN US

It's time to plan your first vision retreat! Make plans for the kids to be cared for and choose a few days when you can get away alone together. Start by submitting your marriage to God in prayer and then address any area of your marriage including: children, finances, careers, sex, and expectations. Write everything down. Talk and pray for half of the time and have fun the other half! Know that God will meet with you and make you one heart and mind in a marriage guided by His wisdom.

GROWING TOGETHER

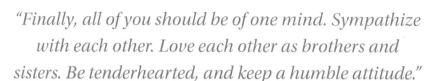

"Finally, all of you should be of one mind. Sympathize with each other. Love each other as brothers and sisters. Be tenderhearted, and keep a humble attitude."

PROVERBS 29:18 (NASB)

In marriage, we have to be intentional about growing together. Even if you have grown apart, you can make a decision to grow back together. The first thing that helps couples grow as partners is to make decisions on faith instead of emotion. Emotions are real, but decisions need to be based on the Bible and what God says.

Couples should have a purpose they accomplish together such as serving God together or building a family together. Growing together in your relationship with Jesus is the most important thing a couple can do. Only God can meet your deepest needs. As you pray together and go to church together, you grow in your partnership.

"As you commit to seeking God individually, also commit to pursuing a committed relationship with a Bible-believing local church and fellow believers." – Jimmy Evans, The Four Laws of Love | Pg.138

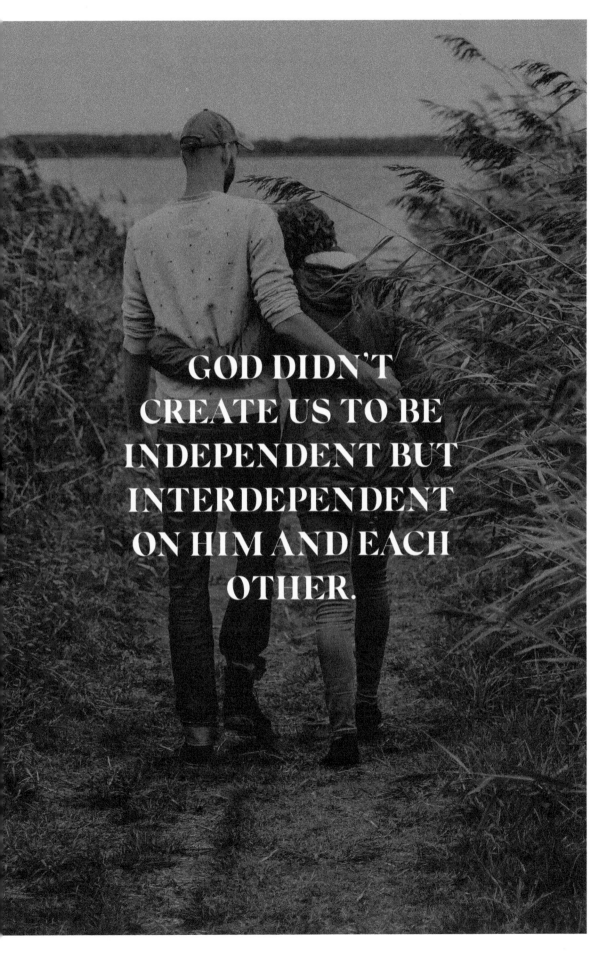

GOD DIDN'T CREATE US TO BE INDEPENDENT BUT INTERDEPENDENT ON HIM AND EACH OTHER.

 Watch "Session 5 - Growing Together " on XO Now.

DISCUSSION QUESTIONS

1. Can you think of a time you made a decision based on emotion? What was the outcome?

2. What does it look like to make decisions on faith vs. fear and how do we know the difference?

3. How can emotions sometimes get in the way of making relational decisions based on the Bible?

4. What are needs that only God can meet in our life? How does it take pressure off your spouse when you go to God for those needs?

5. What are common things that can separate couples, causing them to become independent of one another?

6. What are ways you and your spouse are growing together?

JUST BETWEEN US

Buy a plant and work on taking care of it together! Make a decision to not grow apart but to grow together. Find at least one thing you can do together as a couple regularly that will bring you together to talk, pray and work as a team. Then dream big and proactively pursue this dream together.

DISARMING DESTRUCTIVE DOMINANCE

"For whoever wants to save his life will lose it, but whoever loses his life for me will find it."

MATTHEW 16:25 (NIV)

The law of partnership is absolute in marriage. We must share everything as equals. Dominance in a marriage destroys intimacy and good will. Dominance is disrespectful behavior in a marriage. As human beings, God created us to relate to our spouses as equals. God created us for shared control.

Marriage is a partnership where the two share their lives together as equals. If your spouse is naturally dominating in personality, you must lovingly stand your ground and insist upon respect and consideration. Nothing will change in your marriage if you aren't willing to do your part. A marriage can only flourish when the two are submitted to one another.

"The law of partnership breaks the curse of control off of our marriages and allows us to return to Eden and live together as loving equals. We share life together and make our decisions together without bullying or manipulating to get our way." – Jimmy Evans, The Four Laws of Love | Pg. 120

AS HUMAN
BEINGS, GOD
CREATED US
TO RELATE TO
OUR SPOUSES
AS EQUALS.
CONTROL IS
AGAINST OUR
DESIGN.

Watch "Session 6 – Disarming Destructive Dominance" on XO Now.

DISCUSSION QUESTIONS

1. Did you grow up in a home where one of your parents was clearly dominant over your other parent?

2. Do you believe that dominance had a negative effect on your parents' marriage and the family?

3. Read Matthew 5:33–37. Why is it so wrong for us to make inner vows or to swear to something?

4. Read 1 Samuel 15:23a. Why would the Bible equate stubbornness with the sin of idolatry?

5. Why do you think dominance destroys the intimacy and goodwill of a marriage?

6. Do you feel like you are equal partners in your marriage? If not, what needs to change for this to happen?

JUST BETWEEN US

Each of you choose an area of your marriage where you want to surrender or share control. Share with each other why you want to surrender this area. Then write it down on a piece of paper and actually give it to your spouse. Pray together and trust God to bring unity in your marriage.

DISARMING ANGER

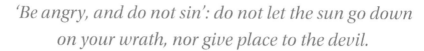

'Be angry, and do not sin': do not let the sun go down
on your wrath, nor give place to the devil.

EPHESIANS 4:26-27 (NKJV)

The law of purity means we can be open both physically, emotionally, and mentally without shame. If you have a good marriage, it doesn't mean you never get angry. It means you can process your anger in a healthy way. We need to be honest about anger. It's okay to be angry and even God gets angry. But we have to deal with our anger in a proper way.

The enemy uses anger to cause offense with our spouse. Resist the devil in your marriage by dealing with unresolved anger. Never go to bed angry. Ask the Holy Spirit to teach you how to be a great spouse, and commit to talking things out regularly with your spouse.

"When you are resolving conflicts with your spouse, you need to admit any fault you have in the situation and ask for their forgiveness. It is important that you both tell each other that you forgive each other and are sincere." – Jimmy Evans, The Four Laws of Love | Pg. 178

MAKE ANGER LEGAL
IN YOUR RELATIONSHIP,
AND DEAL WITH IT
PROPERLY AND WITH
MUTUAL RESPECT.

Watch "Session 7 – Disarming Anger" on XO Now.

DISCUSSION QUESTIONS

1. Growing up, how was anger handled in your home?

2. Is it better for you to express your anger or repress your anger and why?

3. How do you handle anger in your life and in your marriage?

4. Do you agree or disagree that we shouldn't go to bed angry and why?

5. What is one area where you feel like your spouse handles anger in a healthy way? What is one area where you feel like you handle anger in a healthy way?

6. What is one way where you and your spouse can grow in the area of making anger legal and dealing with it in a proper way?

JUST BETWEEN US

Take a relaxing walk together and make a commitment to each other to not go to bed angry. Pray for God to reveal to you any area in your mind or heart where you have believed lies about your spouse. If God reveals an area or a situation, repent to your spouse and ask God to heal your marriage.

RESOLVING CONFLICT IN MARRIAGE

"A soft answer turns away wrath, but a harsh word stirs up anger."

PROVERBS 15:1 (NKJV)

Conflict is inevitable and we have to learn the skills for resolving it. The first step to resolving anger is to admit it and allow everyone else to admit theirs. In a functional relationship, there is a "complaint counter" where you can be honest without fear. There must be an openness in your marriage where your spouse has permission to complain to you so that you can work through conflict.

When you are ready to deal with conflict, start lovingly. The first three minutes of a conversation will dictate the outcome of that conversation. Complain to your spouse, but don't criticize them. Always assume the best about your spouse. Listen to your spouse and believe what they tell you. Be quick to forgive and let the offense go.

"We need to forgive ourselves and our spouses for the mistakes we have made. We also need to put our faith in God to restore our marriages and intimacy." – Jimmy Evans, The Four Laws of Love | Pg. 183

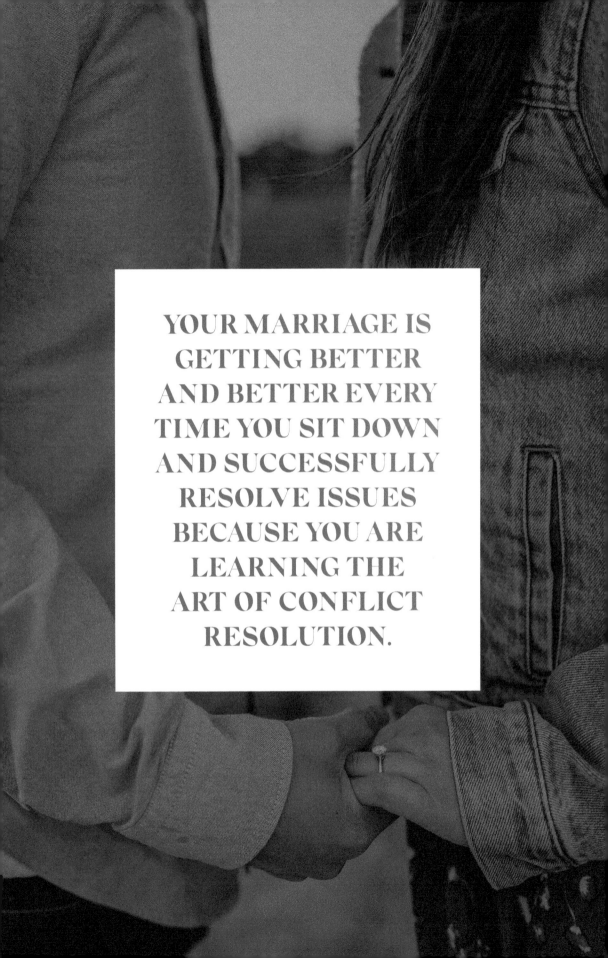

YOUR MARRIAGE IS
GETTING BETTER
AND BETTER EVERY
TIME YOU SIT DOWN
AND SUCCESSFULLY
RESOLVE ISSUES
BECAUSE YOU ARE
LEARNING THE
ART OF CONFLICT
RESOLUTION.

Watch "Session 8 – Resolving Conflict in Marriage" on XO Now.

DISCUSSION QUESTIONS

1. Why do we need to take responsibility when we do something wrong, and what does this communicate to your spouse?

2. How can you create an atmosphere in your marriage where you both have the right to complain without paying a price?

3. How would you want your spouse to approach you with a complaint or how would you like them to complain to you?

4. How did your parents deal with conflict?

5. How are you open or not open to giving and receiving complaints in your marriage?

6. What is the number one issue or reason that you are unable to give or receive complaints?

JUST BETWEEN US

Role model for your spouse what it would look like and sound like for them to lovingly complain to you. Each take a turn on what this would look like. Then, if you are comfortable, lovingly share one way you would like to grow in an area of intimacy in your marriage. After you share, pray together. Ask God to help you to grow in your love and respect for each other and to help you to always be safe places to share complaints and concerns.

"God has a perfect plan for marriage, and there is no plan B. Every marriage can thrive and grow in intimacy and passion for a lifetime."

JIMMY EVANS

Printed in the USA
CPSIA information can be obtained
at www.ICGtesting.com
LVHW071023080824
787692LV00009B/93